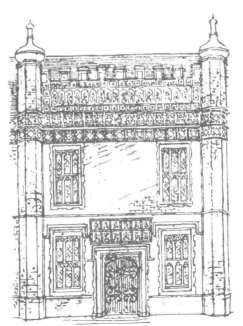

Flower Arrangements in Stately Homes

Julia Clements

FLOWER ARRANGEMENTS IN STATELY HOMES

George Newnes Ltd London

Also by Julia Clements
FUN WITH FLOWERS
PICTURES WITH FLOWERS
MORE PICTURES WITH FLOWERS
101 IDEAS FOR FLOWER ARRANGEMENTS
FIRST STEPS WITH FLOWERS
MY ROSES
FLORAL ROUNDABOUT
PARTY PIECES
FUN WITHOUT FLOWERS
SHOW PIECES
ABC OF FLOWER ARRANGING
COLOUR BOOK OF FLOWER ARRANGEMENTS
BEGINNER'S GUIDE TO FLOWER ARRANGING

Printed in Hungary by
Kossuth Printing House

FRONTISPIECE:—*Longleat House has been described as the most classical house of the English Renaissance. The sumptuous silver that decorates the dining table, notably the massive centrepiece, is complemented by this simple arrangement of red and pink roses. The glowing colours of the flowers help to bring warmth to the glittering table.*

Contents

Acknowledgements

It is a pleasure to record my thanks to the following for so kindly receiving me in their homes, and for giving me facilities to make and to photograph my arrangements.

THE VISCOUNT ASTOR
THE MARQUIS OF BATH
THE LORD MONTAGU OF BEAULIEU
THE DUKE OF BEDFORD
THE DUKE OF DEVONSHIRE
J. PAUL GETTY, ESQ.
THE EARL OF HAREWOOD
THE VISCOUNT DE L'ISLE
THE MARQUIS OF LINLITHGOW
THE DUKE OF MARLBOROUGH
THE DUKE OF NORTHUMBERLAND
LADY PRICE
THE MARQUIS OF SALISBURY
SIR HAROLD WERNHER

and, of course, Jon Whitbourne, who deserves my very real thanks for
his patience and continued interest in taking most of the photographs in
this book.

The book was designed by Tony Kingsnorth

Foreword

Here is the book I have longed for years to make. I love arranging flowers. Even more I love helping others to do so, especially in surroundings that offer inspiration or challenge. In England's stately homes I discovered plenty of both, and nothing has given me greater pleasure than the opportunity to record, in words and in pictures, my experiences as a flower arranger at so many of these great, historic houses.

My eyes were really opened to the possibilities of such a project by people I have met on my travels in various parts of the world. Some while ago, I remember, when talking to American audiences about the history of English gardens, I was constantly asked the same question: How different in style were the flower decorations in some of the famous homes I had mentioned from those then favoured by transatlantic hostesses? Many of these ladies, mainly Garden Club members and already successful flower arrangers, expressed a strong desire to come to England to find out for themselves. In fact the interest was so widespread that I wrote to the British Travel Association which later arranged some special tours. In Australia and New Zealand, also, the subject of flowers in a setting of centuries-old splendour seemed to have an equal fascination. And so the idea for this book was born.

In the course of putting it together I have learned a lot, often through my own mistakes. To begin with, I underestimated the extent of the advance planning—with owners, indoor staff and gardeners—required for each of my visits. I quickly learned, too, to free my mind from any preconceived notions concerning the style of my flower arrangements; for the grandeur and spaciousness of the settings proved, in reality, to be on an even vaster scale than I had imagined from a distance. Adaptability was also essential because I was frequently limited in my choice of flowers and containers. And there were times when, naturally enough, the owner's personal wishes had to be considered.

Many of the beautiful vases I saw, and would have loved to use, were non-functional and kept as treasured ornaments, and I was sometimes the cause of a battle of wills between butler and head-gardener—the former anxious to obtain the best flowers for the rooms, the latter intent on retaining them in herbacious border or greenhouse.

I particularly recall one occasion when, invited by the gardener on a privileged tour of the greenhouses, I noticed pots of exquisite orchids, amaryllis, caladiums and other exotic plants which I felt were far more in keeping with the gorgeous salon I was about to decorate than the flowers that had actually been provided. So, greatly daring, I asked if I might borrow some of these plants for long enough to have them photographed inside the house.

"Oh no, I couldn't bring them indoors," the gardener replied. "The butler would want to keep them there, and his lordship will be visiting the greenhouses tomorrow."

I have said that flower arranging in stately homes offers both inspiration and challenge. And indeed, at each one of them I encountered almost an *embarras de richesse*. Surrounded as I was with so much elegance and grace, the challenge was in trying to create with flowers a living picture that would not only echo the beauty of its setting but, if possible, enhance it.

Conditioned as we are to the tempo of modern life, it takes time, of course, to absorb the atmosphere of a more gracious and leisured age. Often and often, after completing a day's work and leaving a great house, I longed to go back, to stand and stare once more and, with different flowers, to begin all over again.

There was inspiration everywhere for lavish and lofty arrangements. Yet I think it was the small treasures that touched my imagination most vividly: a jewelled cigarette box; a clock encrusted with diamonds and pearls; a gold-footed Venetian glass goblet which seemed made for a trail of honey-suckle; a Sèvres china ladle in which I longed to place just one perfect rose....

Looking back on it all now, I realize that I have been able to reproduce in this book only a glimpse of the enchantment that awaits the fortunate visitor to England's stately homes. But I hope that the following pages will help to persuade others to go, as I did, to see these treasure-houses for themselves.

I have acknowledged their owners by name elsewhere. But I would like to say 'thank you' here for the kindness and co-operation my photographer and I received. I would like, also, to remind all those who have yet to enjoy the pleasure of visiting these wonderful places that nowhere else in the world is such an abundance of unsurpassed beauty to be found.

Chelsea, London   JULIA CLEMENTS

Introduction

Nobody really knows when the idea of using flowers for indoor decoration, as distinct from growing them in gardens, was first introduced into English homes. But a Dutchman called Levinus Lemnius, writing about his visit to England in the year 1560, referred to "nosegays finely intermingled with sundry sorts of fragraunte flowers in their bedchambers and privy rooms". So at least we know that the art of flower arranging in England is over 400 years old.

Those 16th century nosegays "entirely delighted" the Dutchman who, making comparisons with home-life in his own country, went on to say: "Altho we trimme up our rooms with green boughes and vine leaves, no nation does it more decently nor more sightly than they doe in Englande." But it seems doubtful whether our choice of flowers was as wide as it is today.

Nearly a century later, when an edition of herbalist John Gerard's *Herball* (based on the earlier work of a French botanist) appeared with two arrangements of garden flowers pictured on the frontispiece, John Parkinson, a well known horticulturist and botanist of the time, described as "outlandish" several of the varieties shown. He did not recognise them, for they were not then known in England.

Later still, in 1670, John Evelyn, the celebrated diarist, noted: "Lord Stafford, who disliked roses, rose from the Dinner table in some disorder because there were roses stuck among the fruite when the dessert came in and was set upon the table." Fascinating to find that our modern-style fruit and flower decorations were already in use in the reign of Charles the Second.

Philip Miller, compiler of *The Gardeners' Dictionary* published in London in the 1730's, mentioned that the beautiful flower-heads of globe amaranth *(Gomphrena globusa)* will last for several years in the house if gathered before they are too far advanced. Reference to the dry flowers of statice, "making a pretty wintertime ornament for the mantelpiece", was also to be found in Curtis's Botanical Magazine of the 18th century. Thus began the vogue for dry flower decoration which has continued down to the present day.

Very little seems to have been written about flowers in the house during early Georgian times, though Thomas Fairchild, author of *The City Gardener*, gave a list of flowers and evergreens that would thrive in London, adding: "one may guess the general love my fellow citizens have in gardening and furnishing their chambers with basins of flowers and boughpots rather than not have something of a garden before them." In fact, it was just at this period that the great potter, Josiah Wedgwood, was producing jardinieres, bulb-bowls, boughpots and other plant containers. Presumably, however, these were mainly intended for ornamental shrubs or foliage rather than for cut flowers; for in the years between 1714 and 1760 many of the largest and most fashionable gardens became almost totally devoid of floral displays.

The probable explanation is not far to seek. This was the heyday of landscape gardening, the new craze which transformed walled-in gardens, crisscrossed by dividing hedges, into wide-open, sweeping expanses of lawns and terraces, winning fame and fortune for a gardener named Lancelot Brown. Known as "Capability" Brown, because of his habit of declaring that a garden had "great capabilities", he became far and away the most sought-after landscaping expert in England and was employed all over the country to remodel acres of parks and grounds belonging to large estates. Brown's idea was to bring the countryside right up to the house by demolishing fences and knocking down walls. It was he who introduced, instead, the ha-ha boundary ditches, many of which are still in existence today, to avoid obscuring the view. These ditches, or sunken fences, are thought to have acquired their curious name from the surprised exclamation given by people who suddenly came across them when out walking and found their progress so unexpectedly checked.

The fame of Capability Brown eventually spread to the other side of the English Channel and even to Russia. To own *un jardin anglais* soon became the ambition of all the owners of great houses in Europe. But this led, for a while, to the almost total disappearance of cultivated flowers. Flowerbeds, ruled Brown, would have spoiled the pastoral effect of his natural vistas.

By the beginning of the Victorian era, however, the landscape gardener was superceded by the topiarist whose clippers once again revived the Tudor-type formality of trimmed hedges and shaped yew. At the same time there was a swing back to flowers. Planted in beds geometrically laid out with gravel paths between, they filled the terraces in front of large houses with blaze upon blaze of dazzling colour.

Early in Queen Victoria's reign, the making of posies—tight little bunches of small, sweet-scented spring or summer flowers—was one of the essential accomplishments of fashionable young ladies who seldom attended a social function without one. Usually embellished with a surrounding frill of real or paper lace, these posies were carried about in special, trumpet-shaped holders, often made of silver, which allowed water to reach the flower stems when placed in a tall vase. And this, no doubt, was the origin of the posy style for small flower arrangements which has remained popular ever since.

The Victorian lady also learned to make artificial flowers out of feathers and wax to use as a decoration under a glass dome. In her garden she sowed flower seeds in patterns, choosing the most brilliantly coloured blooms, and her gardener carefully bedded out plants to produce the most striking contrasts in tone and hue. Devotees of *The Lady's Book*, a mid-Victorian fashion magazine, were advised: "There is no doubt that arranging flowers according to contrast, or their complementary colours, is more pleasing to the eye than placing them according to their harmonies. Therefore a blue flower should be placed next to an orange one, whilst red or white flowers should have abundant foliage near them."

Reading this, one is reminded of the blue lobelia, yellow calceolaria and red geranium flower-bed schemes of a hundred years ago—a far cry from the much more melodious grouping preferred in our arrangements today. For years, now, English flower arrangers have been known all over the world as experts in the blending of harmonious colours, and I have often wondered if this may be due to the softening effect of our grey skies, or whether we owe this reputation to the influence of William Robinson and his introduction of the wild, or natural, garden at the turn of the century. Many other gardeners followed Robinson's lead, and towards the end of the Victorian age there was far less formality in plant-bedding. Gradually, as a larger variety of different plants found their way into our gardens, and hardy cottage flowers like lupins, hollyhocks, delphiniums, antirrhinums and Canterbury bells began to share the garden with more sophisticated species, the herbaceous border came into being and is now a feature of most gardens of any size—especially where cut flowers are regularly used for decorating the owner's house.

The gardens of England's stately homes are well worth visiting on their own account, the majority being just as full of historic interest and atmosphere as the great houses themselves. For in spite of changing fashions down the centuries and generations of innumerable different gardeners, these gardens retain a great deal of their original character and design.

In the grounds of Hatfield House, Hertfordshire, for instance, are some of the oldest mulberry trees in England. Planted by King James I, they were grown to feed the silk-worms that produced the silk from which the court robes were made. At Syon House, Middlesex, there is a superb specimen of the rare liquidambar tree as well as the largest number of ancient oaks to be found on one estate anywhere in the country. And great clumps of every known variety of rhododendron and azalea may be studied and admired at Bodnant, in North Wales, Exbury, in Hampshire, and at Leonardslee and Nymans, in Sussex. Nymans has the mighty *Rhododendron sino-grande*, the leaves of which, when fully mature, are up to two feet long. Then there is the Tudor-style knot garden which can be seen at Hampton Court, Middlesex, and at Birr Castle, in Ireland; and fine examples of topiary work (yews close-clipped into decorative shapes) still stand like sentinels at Hutton John in Cumberland, Leven Hall in Westmorland, Compton Wyngates in Warwickshire and Chilham Castle in Kent—to name but a few places, for there are many more.

In various parts of the country, too, there are gardens containing pleached alleys, dating back to the 16th century and mentioned by Shakespeare in *Much Ado About Nothing*. These shady walks were formed with trees such as witch elms, willows, hornbeams or limes, their branches so impleached, or plaited, as to provide shelter from the sun for Elizabethan ladies 'taking the air'. An excellent example can be seen at Sissinghurst, in Kent.

The parks and gardens belonging to our great national heritage of architectural treasures and noble homes can be enjoyed as much for their visual beauty as for their botanical or historical interest. But it is sometimes felt, perhaps, that something of their former glory has been lost. Gone are the days when there would have been forty gardeners. Few houses now will have more than six, or eight at the very most. Even then, in some instances, much of the garden produce is sold commercially. Unfortunately, too, the old type of head gardener is becoming very rare. He was the high priest of the hot house, the lord of the rosebeds, using his skill and artistry to produce for a weekend house-party or a State visit a different dinner-table flower scheme at every meal. The rarity of the blooms and plants he displayed was evidence of his master's wealth. Now, on special occasions, a professional florist may sometimes be called in.

Yet skilful arrangements of flowers are still an important ingredient of the grace and charm in the great homes that now rely largely on the visiting public for their upkeep and support. Always there are plants and flowers on display, not only in the public rooms but in the private ones.

During the last war, when the 'Dig for Britain' campaign stripped gardens of their flowers to make way for vegetables to feed the nation, we became starved of beauty and colour. As a result, there was an almost passionate return to flower-gardening and floral decoration in our homes as soon as the war was over. From this, I think, has stemmed the tremendous growth of interest in the art of flower arranging, which now attracts millions all over the world. And it has become apparent that visitors love to see flowers in the beautiful settings of our stately homes.

To satisfy this demand, many famous houses have opened their doors to members of Flower Clubs, of which there are a very large number in Britain. Recently, wonderful displays have been staged for charity by Flower Club members at such houses as Longleat (South West Area Clubs), Montacute (Dorset Clubs), Clandon (Surrey Clubs), Newby Hall and Harewood House (Yorkshire Clubs), Blenheim Palace (Bedfordshire, Buckinghamshire and Oxfordshire Clubs) and others in various parts of the country.

These displays have shown how imaginative and talented Flower Club members have become, and how advanced many of them are in the study of floral art. Their arrangements have attracted vast crowds to the great houses whose rooms they have decorated, and the skill of the arrangers has often matched the artistry of the furniture designer and the portrait painter whose work their flowers have complemented.

Speaking, as I now can, from personal experience, I know that flower arranging against such backgrounds as these poses special problems seldom encountered elsewhere. The richness of the furnishings and ornaments, the tapestries and paintings adorning the walls and, above all, the spaciousness of the rooms with their immensely high ceilings—all this adds up to the sort of setting that calls for an entirely different approach from that of normal procedure and practice when designing arrangements for an average-sized home.

One's eye must first take in the dimensions and teach the mind to think big and bold. Magnificence must be matched to magnificence. Colour must glow against colour. And many more flowers are needed when one takes a second and third look.

Through trial and error I eventually discovered that colour, rather than strict design, was the key to the most effective results. I found, too, that, in most of the stately homes I visited, massed flowers with plenty of height and arranged in a loose, flowing style were far more successful than something small or intricate. With so many treasures to compete with, anything too precise tends to get lost, and arrangements can easily be eight feet tall without looking in the least overpowering.

Containers need careful thought. Best of all for my purpose was the type which is wider at the top than at the base—such as the wide fluted bowls on footed stands which I found myself using continually. These can be placed almost anywhere with ease; on side tables, perhaps, or, to achieve extra height, on tall pedestals.

It naturally helps if you happen to be knowledgeable about the various techniques of keeping your container steady and making your flowers stay put. For very tall arrangements, I often placed heavy stones in the bottom of the vase to weight it down as a first step, then added crumpled wire netting placed firmly down inside and rising in a cone shape well above the rim as an extra support for the central stems. Crumpled wire is excellent, too, for holding the side and shorter front stems just over the rim, allowing them to curve down to the water.

Growing in a garden, as I have said, flowers are ends in themselves, each to be admired individually for its own sake. But when cut and brought into a house to form a decoration, they become a means to an end. Now it is the overall design that is of chief importance, and to this every flower that takes part in it plays a subservient role. Like musicians in an orchestra, each is instrumental to the symphony of the whole. For, like music that lifts the heart and delights the ear with the sound of beauty, a flower arrangement should be a lovely blend of shape, texture and colour. The flower arranger, of course, is the conductor who decides which notes to stress and which to subdue.

Like music, like painting, or like dancing ... flower arranging seems to combine aspects of many other arts in a particularly subtle yet satisfying way. As a painter completes his picture with touches of white for highlights and dark patches for shadows to obtain a three-dimensional effect, so a skilled flower arranger highlights a design with silvery grasses and adds dark leaves for depth. And just as a dancer weaves patterns of movement or stands poised in an arabesque, so will a flower arranger strive for fluid lines and ballerina grace.

A flower arrangement anywhere can be as eloquent as poetry, as evocative as bird-song. It can also become, quite unconsciously, an expression of the arranger's own personality. But in all the stately homes I visited, my aim was to create arrangements that would not only echo the richness of the setting and the glories of the past but speak, too, of the living present—of the warmth and intimacy sensed in any house that is also a well-loved home. And, whenever possible, I relied for my materials on what could be provided by the surrounding garden, so that visitors passing between house and grounds would find in my flowers a natural link between the two.

Whether satisfied or not with a completed arrangement—is one ever entirely so?—one likes to feel that it will give pleasure to as many as possible for as long as possible. Looking around, pondering on the problems of decorating large rooms, I have come to the conclusion that, in many such settings, dry flower arrangements could be a happy solution, both economically and physically. Not only are they beautiful to look at but they require very little attention and stay looking attractive for a long time. And where there are extensive grounds, there is always, of course, a wealth of plant material which could be used for this purpose. Leaves could be preserved in glycerine and water, seed-heads gathered and brighter flowers preserved with silica gel or borax—the results lasting for several months.

I have fully described all the methods of flower and foliage preservation in my book: *101 Ideas For Flower Arrangement**. But as I was using fresh flowers for the designs featured in this book, I have included at the end a few suggestions for prolonging the life of mixed flower displays, together with diagrams of the basic build-up of some of the arrangements shown in the photographs.

Incidentally, I find it easier to position my container first, in the place where the flowers are to stand, and do the arrangement on the spot to avoid the risk of disturbing it afterwards. For this reason, I always have handy a large sheet of polythene in which to carry the flowers to the vase and to cover the surrounding floor while I work. I make sure, of course, that there is a glass or cork mat beneath the vase to protect the furniture—vitally important in other people's homes, particularly when it happens to be priceless, unique and irreplaceable.

By now, perhaps, I have said enough to convince even those who are not specially interested in flower arranging that the great houses, which in-

* G. Arthur Pearson, Ltd.

spired so many of my own efforts, offer a multitude of delights to all who find their way to them. And they can be sure of a welcome on visiting days. For apart from the National Trust—an organisation supported by its members for the preservation of land and buildings—there is no way of meeting the ever-rising costs of maintaining these vast houses and grounds other than opening them to a paying public. Nevertheless, some people have told me that they have a sense of intrusion on entering, even of gross impertinence at being, in this modern age, among "the first invaders".

But this is not so. Visiting private property was a popular pastime four centuries ago when, without invitation and through sheer curiosity, people in polite society would suddenly descend on the country residences of complete strangers and expect to be shown round the house and gardens. This fashion is believed to have been started by Queen Elizabeth I who, always inquisitive about the homes of her more well-to-do subjects, would frequently announce that she wished to visit a certain house. She would then proceed, on arrival, to examine all their possessions and demand a room to be prepared for her in which to stay the night—a habit which no doubt accounts for the large number of beds that Elizabeth is alleged to have slept in.

Today, the owners of these houses and monuments still observe the time-honoured tradition of welcoming the strangers at their gates. The only real difference is that they are now forced to charge an entrance fee. These modern visitors, however, unlike their non-paying predecessors, have the satisfaction of knowing that they are not only contributing to the support of these beautiful homes but enabling their hosts and hostesses to remain in occupation.

This is surely the great hidden asset of England's stately homes, the value of which should never be forgotten or disregarded. Unlike so many of the show-places in other countries, these great houses are not impersonal, dehumanised museums but still lived in and warm with life. You can walk into a room and feel, as I have felt, that one of the family has just walked out. For there, on a table, is a bowl of flowers or a book, perhaps from the library shelves, or a family photograph grouped with others bearing royal signatures of our own century . . . .

Such things can never be measured except in terms of love—the kind of love with which this book has been made.

Blenheim Palace

Lush meadows, tall trees, a majestic bridge, a shimmering lake ... seen suddenly, for the first time, in this lovely pastoral setting, Blenheim Palace has a quality of unreality—almost of fantasy—about it. One can only stand and stare.

The birthplace of Sir Winston Churchill, this great stone house, built in Woodstock Park, Oxfordshire, was a gift from Queen Anne to Sir Winston's illustrious ancestor, the first Duke of Marlborough, to commemorate his defeat of Louis XIV at the battle of Blenheim in 1704. Certainly its architect, Sir John Vanbrugh, spared neither patience nor expense to achieve a national monument of such magnificence as to rival the French king's own palace at Versailles.

To create his masterpiece, he employed the best artists and craftsmen in the country, among them the world-famous sculptor and carver, Grinling Gibbons, whose work is everywhere apparent. The result remains a supreme example of English baroque architecture; but it took the best part of twenty years to complete and the costs far exceed the generous sum originally granted by Queen Anne.

It is sad to think that the gallant Duke, suffering from ill-health and forced to dig deep into his own pocket to settle outstanding accounts, scarcely lived long enough to enjoy the rewards of victory, and that Sarah, his Duchess, disliked living there. Stone, she complained, was bad for her gout, and she much preferred her London residence.

The Duke's descendents, however, have always been proud of their inheritance. Blenheim Palace has been their home down to the present day and is now owned by the tenth Duke of Marlborough who has carefully preserved its historic atmosphere.

Wandering from the Red Drawing Room to the Long Gallery, from the Dining Room to the Great Hall and then back to the Chapel, one almost expects to come across elegant figures in powdered wigs and 18th century costumes strolling along the corridors and to hear the strains of a minuet. And I, who had come to say it with flowers, gazed at the priceless treasures around me and realized that here was a challenge indeed. How could I hope to echo with my flowers even so much as a whisper of all this grandeur and grace?

Except for the terrace and formal garden on the East Front, laid out by the ninth Duke of Marlborough in 1920, the grounds have remained largely unchanged since Capability Brown remodelled them in his own landscape style 200 years ago. Sweeping away Vanbrugh's parterre, planting trees and constructing the lake from a stream, Brown gave Blenheim what countless admirers have described as the finest view in England.

Water, wood, stone ... these are the imperishable ingredients of the glory that is Blenheim.

Blenheim: — The Palace lies eight miles north of Oxford on the A34 road on the outskirts of Woodstock.

LEFT: *In the chapel, yellow and white flowers in the pulpit, which is only six feet in width, and tends to emphasise the strength of the Rysbrack memorial which is twenty-four feet high. The tomb, designed by William Kent as a memorial to the First Duke, his Duchess and two sons, is carved in marble.*

Blenheim Palace

ABOVE: *Close up of the gold centrepiece, presented by King Edward VII when Prince of Wales, showing fruit, lilac and cherry blossom in the two-tiered stands, the centre epergne holding camellias in each cup. Notice how both the colours and the design of the arrangement complements its surroundings.*

RIGHT: *The murals and painted ceilings in the Saloon are the work of Louis Laguerre (1663–1721). Also in this magnificent room as you can see the marble doorcases, one of which was set up by Grinling Gibbons. After the Duchess's quarrel with Queen Anne all building was stopped, and it was not until the accession of George I that work proceeded again—but at the Duke's expense.*

Blenheim Palace

LEFT: *At the end of the Red Drawing Room hangs the famous painting by Sargent of the 9th Duke, with his Duchess and family. The young boy in the yellow satin suit is the present Duke. Flowers in crimson and pink were placed on the transitional Louis XV writing table.*

LEFT: *Here is a close up of the arrangement shown in the previous picture. Crimson amaryllis, antirrhinums and solomon's seal, flow along the planes of the Louis XV writing table, emphasised in the centre with pink pelargoniums, orchids and azaleas which blend with the background.*

RIGHT: *This ornate yet beautiful copy of a Venetian cradle was given to Consuelo Vanderbilt, the American wife of the 9th Duke, by her mother, on the occasion of the birth of the present Duke. On it rests a posy of lilies of the valley and pinks. Over the mantelpiece hangs a portrait painted in Paris by Carolus Duran of Consuelo Vanderbilt when she was 17 years old.*

RIGHT: *This charming bronze, of the present Duke aged nine months, was cast by Emile Fuchs. The arrangement, which reflects the lines of the figure, is built up with lime green nicotiana (tobacco flowers) at the centre, and pink carnations and red roses flowing out.*

Blenheim Palace

LEFT: *A close up of the huge jewel box, shown opposite, in which I placed a container, filled with wire netting to hold the heavy flowers in place. This large arrangement of peonies, lilacs and tulips, harmonises beautifully with the soft colours of the tapestries hanging behind it.*

RIGHT: *This beautiful jewel box and the clock cabinet are both early 18th century examples of the work of the famous French cabinet maker, Charles André Bouille. The clock itself was made by Gavdon Apans. The tapestry in the background depicts the Battle of Oudenarde fought in 1708.*

LEFT: *Detail of the East Gate.*

22

Luton Hoo

Few British country houses that are opened to the public can show an international art collection as superb as that to be found at Luton Hoo, the Bedfordshire home of Sir Harold Wernher and his wife, Lady Zia. Unlike the majority of stately homes, however, the house as it stands today is barely 120 years old, and its priceless contents have been assembled only during the last three decades.

Hoo is a Saxon word meaning the spur of a hill, and though there has been a manor house on this site, near Luton, at least since the 13th century, the original building has long since ceased to exist. After many alterations and changes of ownership, the Luton Hoo house that was the home of the Marquis of Bute was almost entirely destroyed by fire in 1843, together with all that remained of its transformation by Robert Adam in the previous century. Subsequently rebuilt from the ruins by a wealthy Liverpool solicitor named John Leigh, Luton Hoo was later sold, in 1903, to Sir Harold's father, Sir Julius Wernher, who redesigned the architecture, redecorated the interior in the French style of the period and turned it into the treasure house that it is today.

Both Sir Harold's mother and his wife have made their own, individual contributions to its glories—Lady Wernher having owned the marvellous collection of English porcelain, and Lady Zia, who is descended from Nicholas I of Russia, bringing an inheritance of fabulous jewelled ornaments fashioned by Fabergé, jeweller to the two last Tsars.

Over the last twenty years, Sir Harold and Lady Zia have made further additions to the art treasures—notably several Dutch paintings and some beautiful old pieces of furniture—and provided wonderful display settings to delight the visiting public.

But if the present house can no longer lay claim to an historic past, the surroundings still bear witness to the 18th century handiwork of the ubiquitous Capability Brown who landscaped the grounds as you see them today. It was Brown who damned up the River Lea to create the two lakes and who used the woodlands and park as a scenic background to spacious lawns. But the colourful effect achieved by the beautiful formal garden is due to Lady Zia's own passionate interest in flowers.

It is she who plans the schemes for the flower-beds, and the lovely hybrid tea-rose named after her has, of course, a special place among them. I particularly admired her idea of placing huge stone urns beneath the great cedar trees on the lawns and filling them with begonias which, on the day of my visit, were in full bloom and making brilliant splashes of colour.

A week earlier, Luton Hoo had been the scene of a ball given for Her Majesty the Queen; and I only wished, as I chose the flowers for my own arrangement in the house, that I had been in time to photograph the great masses of blue hydrangeas and delphiniums that had been used to decorate the blue hall for the occasion.

Luton Hoo: — Luton Hoo may be reached from the A6 at Luton, Bedfordshire.

LEFT: *Many of Luton Hoo's famous tapestries can be seen in the Blue Hall, especially that of the Chancellerie, woven at the Gobelins factory about 1770. The visitor will see also a collection of the outstanding work of Carl Fabergé. My picture shows a long design of blue campanulas and roses placed on a marble-topped French table below two hanging tapestries.*

Luton Hoo

ABOVE: *The south side of the house from the rose garden. Adam, the original architect, was responsible for this front, and it was left as he designed it until the early 20th century, when it was rebuilt as we see it today. The rose garden, together with the formal garden, was laid out in the 19th century.*

RIGHT: *Roses, honeysuckle and clematis picked from the garden tumble from the cut crystal centrepiece on the dining table. Most of the gold plate and crystal in this room is of royal origin, some of it Russian. The flowers, rising from the sparkling container, the glittering golden desert service, the softly glowing table and the coruscating chandelier combine with the rich tapestries to give an atmosphere of civilised and restrained splendour.*

LEFT: *Hydrangeas massed in a huge Chinese bowl are here reflected in mirrors in another corner of the Blue Hall. Notice how the soft colours blend in with the decorations and are complemented by the vase in the foreground.*

RIGHT: *Branches of lime-green maple formed the triangular pattern of this arrangement on a green marble pedestal. Euphorbia, roses and lilies placed centrally completed the design. Notice again how the soft colours of the arrangement harmonise with the cabinet and the floor, stand out from the wall yet do not clash with the design on the wallpaper.*

LEFT: *This is the famous Gobelins tapestry, called Chancellerie, worked with the arms of France and Navarre, and in the corners, those of the Duc de la Vrillière, Foreign Minister to King Louis XV. It is hung in the Blue Hall.*

Hatfield House

Sit beneath an oak tree in the grounds of Hatfield House, and you could be sitting in the self-same spot where the young Elizabeth I sat reading her Testament on the day she first knew she was going to be Queen of England. Walk into the Old Palace in the Western Gardens for lunch or tea and you will find yourself in the Banquet Hall of Elizabeth's home, where she held her first Privy Council.

Here, too, are the great mulberry trees planted by James I, and Mary, Queen of Scots was imprisoned in the house that has been the Hertfordshire home of the Cecils for 350 years.

Robert Cecil, first Earl of Salisbury, built it at the start of the 17th century; and as you approach, it is easy to imagine that time has stood still since then, for its outward appearance has scarcely changed.

It was by the invitation of the present Marquis and Marchioness of Salisbury, both of whom take an immense personal interest in the gardens, that I had the pleasure of arranging flowers in such an historic setting. At the time of my visit the herbacious borders were in full and glorious bloom. But first, before choosing the flowers for the James I Pink Room, I lost myself among the twisting paths and close-clipped hedges of the maze, while I thought about colour-schemes.

Long sprays of powder-blue, flowering ceonothus combined with pink roses, perhaps.... Or should it be pink with white buddlea? Once picked, their lower leaves stripped away and their stems re-cut, all the flowers were stood in deep water while I toured the rest of the house.

Its huge marble hall is a Jacobean adaptation of the traditional mediaeval style, with a Minstrels' Gallery and an oriel window; and every room is full of priceless treasures. One that specially entranced me is the posset set presented as a betrothal gift to Philip of Spain and Mary of England by the Spanish Ambassador of the day. Kitchen equipment for preparing soothing hot drinks? A somewhat homely gift, you might think, for a royal pair. But this is no ordinary posset set. Attributed to the world-famous 16th century Italian goldsmith, Benvenuto Cellini, it is fashioned in crystal mounted on gold exquisitely ornamented with enamel and set with precious stones.

Chairs covered in Italian silk date back to the reign of James II; and among other fascinating antiquities is a portrait of Queen Elizabeth I with ermine on her sleeve—a symbol of royalty—painted by Nicholas Hilliard, her court miniaturist.

Before I left I went again into the garden to stand in reverence before the great copper beech trees planted by the wife of the fifth Earl of Salisbury 250 years ago. So old, so beautiful, so rare are the wonders of Hatfield House that the busy, bustling modern world just beyond its gates seems as remote as a distant planet.

Hatfield House:— The House is in Hatfield, Hertfordshire, just opposite the railway station.

LEFT: *The King James Drawing Room, one of the finest rooms in this lovely Jacobean House, owes its name to the statue of the King which stands over the mantelpiece. This was presented to Robert Cecil, First Earl of Salisbury, by James himself. The magnificent family portraits which cover the walls are examples of the work of many of the most famous English artists, notably Romney, Reynolds and Lawrence.*

Hatfield House

LEFT: *I picked this large group of flowers, white hollyhocks, buddleia and pink phlox in the historic grounds, and arranged them simply on a gilt pedestal in the corner of the King James Drawing Room. As I worked, I thought of the unfortunate children of Henry VIII, almost all of whom were imprisoned at Hatfield for some part of their lives. An atmosphere of court politics still seems to be present.*

LEFT: *Detail above the doorway.*

ABOVE: *The Dining Room, one of the many state rooms. Hatfield, when it was built, was almost a survival from an earlier age in that Lord Salisbury planned his house round a great Hall, an enduring feature of mediaeval country houses. In early times it was thought necessary to have one large room to entertain and feed the whole family, staff, visitors and their suites. After this period, less emphasis was placed on huge, draughty banqueting halls and comparatively intimate rooms were built, and the house planned more for convenience than state entertaining.*

LEFT: *White and pastel coloured flowers make this arrangement stand out against the dark, heavy Jacobean background. I used white delphiniums, and philadelphus for the outline, and pale pink floribunda roses to fill in. Green ash foliage contrasted with the soft colours, and the whole brought a beautiful highlight to the otherwise sombre and stately room.*

Hatfield House

LEFT: *This arrangement was set below the large classical vase, to balance it and link it to the flanking gilt and porcelain vases. The pink and white roses, the golden artificial flowers and the classical symmetry of the vases contrast very vividly with the Jacobean panelling and the polished console table that supports the group.*

LEFT: *I massed these brilliant yellow flowers in a bowl on the refectory table in the huge Marble Hall. This room was then a modification of the Great Hall of the mediaeval house. The long table matches perfectly the glowing panelling and intricate carving which embellishes this room. The picture in the left background is the famous Ermine Portrait of the first Queen Elizabeth.*

RIGHT: *Looking down the Marble Hall towards the fretted Minstrels' Gallery. The floor and the painted ceiling are Victorian innovations, but the rest of the room is a perfect example of Jacobean interior decoration, unaltered from the day it was built. The portrait at the end, by Oudry, is of the tragic Mary, Queen of Scots, and is the last to be painted of her before her execution.*

Longleat

Set among Wiltshire's gentle green hills, the great Elizabethan house of Longleat looks as though it has always been there. Since it was first built nearly 400 years ago, this has been the home of the Thynne family—loved and lived in as it still is today. Nevertheless, it has an awe-inspiring magnificence that makes you want to talk in whispers as if entering a cathedral.

Although almost none of the original furniture remains, most of it dates far back to the time of Charles II when the first Lord Weymouth discovered that he had inherited an empty house. That was in 1682, just 100 years after the death of Longleat's founder, Sir John Thynne. In the centuries that followed, succeeding generations added their own enrichments, in particular the fourth Marquis of Bath who, during Queen Victoria's reign, engaged John Crace, a celebrated artist of the day, to design the redecoration of many of the ceilings of the house in Italian Renaissance style.

Skilled craftsmen from Italy were brought to Longleat to carry out this exacting task, and it is well worth a stiff neck to look up and gaze long at these glowing heights, gorgeously gilded, painted and embossed.

Like the house, the garden and grounds have lived through many changes of style and taste. The rural simplicity favoured by Sir John Thynne became, in the early 18th century, fashionably formal when the first Lord Weymouth transformed it with elaborate parterres and ornamental fountains. But the second Lord Weymouth took no interest in maintaining all this, and his son later employed the famous landscaper, Capability Brown, to remodel the whole of the neglected garden and park. The result, with lakes made by Brown from a stream—the Long Leat—and lovely groupings of trees, was much as you see it today, though the present owner, Henry Frederick Thynne, the sixth Marquis of Bath, has restored a great deal of the garden's former ornamental aspect.

Here, for the Great Hall of Longleat, I picked delphiniums five feet high, but even these were dwarfed by the oak-panelled walls rising another 30 feet. Halfway up, at the head of the Grand Staircase, is the original Minstrel's Gallery, and in the King's Bedroom stands the great canopied bed occupied by a series of royal visitors, among them the Duke of Windsor when he was Prince of Wales in 1923. Queen Elizabeth slept in this room in 1574, and among other royal guests at Longleat have been Charles II and Queen Catharine, George III and Queen Charlotte and Edward VII and Queen Alexandra.

I was fascinated, too, in the Robes Corridor, by a display of the favourite dresses of some of the former ladies of Longleat, including the wedding gown worn by the third Marchioness of Bath in the year 1830. These silken dresses seemed so much more in keeping with their gracious surroundings than are the fashions of the present day.

Longleat House:— Longleat House, near Warminster, Wiltshire, may be reached either from Frome or Warminster.

LEFT: *Here delphiniums and paeonies were placed in a large bronze bowl on the original long oak shuffleboard table in the Great Hall. This is one of the only rooms to stay unaltered since the 16th century, when Longleat was built. The picture of two stallions fighting is by John Wootton, and was painted in 1740. Through the open doors of the balcony the visitor can see part of the Italian ornamented ceiling of the State Drawing Room, decorated in the Veronese manner.*

Longleat

LEFT: *A closer view of my arrangement for the Great Hall. The leaves, delphiniums, and paeonies were held in the bronze bowl by crumpled wire netting, pushed down into the receptacle. As I worked, I was impressed by the contrast of the simple, carved beams and plain surfaces of the Great Hall with the elaborate gilding and colour work of the other staterooms.*

RIGHT: *Detail of the entrance to Longleat.*

RIGHT: *Unfortunately, apart from the Great Hall, there are not many of the original Elizabethan features left inside the house. In 1860, the fourth Marquis imported a team of Italian decorators to remodel all the reception rooms, including the State Drawing Room, shown here. I used only pastel shades in this arrangement, which otherwise would not have contrasted with the profusion of rich colours of Titian's 'Holy Family' masterpiece and the elaborate decorations.*

LEFT: *This simple design of crimson pinks was placed in a white bisque urn, supported by charming representations of garlanded cherubs. The glowing tones of the pinks highlight effectively the rich leather bindings and gilt decorations of the books that line the walls of Longleat's famous library.*
Books, particularly old books, make a perfect background for almost any arrangement.

BELOW: *This huge, gilded Chinese porcelain footed container, standing beside the State Drawing Room chimneypiece, held a large rubber plant. Purple Japanese iris were added to give the* pot et fleur *effect. The fireplace is typical of the Italianate decoration imposed on this house.*

ABOVE: *The State Dining Room has been the scene of many sparkling occasions, the first being Queen Elizabeth I's visit in 1574. King Charles II and Catherine of Braganza were also visitors, and so was King George III, with the Queen and three Princesses. I was asked to keep the flowers low so as not to detract from the massive silver centrepiece, yet there were four dozen pinks in each of the tureens on either side of it.*

RIGHT: *I grouped this arrangement of fruit and flowers on a marble topped ormolu trimmed table, standing against richly brocaded wallpaper. This background needed a white, purple, pink and green colour scheme, so I laid fruit across a mound of wire netting placed over a low dish of water. The pink roses and white lilies were then pushed through the wire into the water, and finished with a backing of vine leaves.*

41

Woburn Abbey

When John Russell, the 13th Duke of Bedford, inherited Woburn Abbey in 1953, together with a debt of £5,000,000 for death duties, he might well have felt that 13 was an unlucky number for him. Instead, with his natural optimism, he decided to "go commercial" and make his ancestral home at Woburn, Bedfordshire, the most popular show place in Britain.

Open to the public all the year round, the Abbey, with its 3,000 acres of beautiful park, including a zoo, now attracts thousands of visitors, and the Duke and his lovely French wife work hard to entertain them. A restaurant is provided for those in need of refreshment, and the great house, with its multitude of treasures, is always warm and welcoming.

It was by the invitation of the Duchess herself that I journeyed there to spend an unforgettable day exploring and admiring. Everything, I noticed, was in excellent condition—cared for and cherished. No one could have guessed, I thought, that it had not always been like this; that Woburn, officially occupied during the second world war, had been left in a state of chaos; and that, on coming into his inheritance, the Duke had renovated and restored it in the short space of six months, creating the delight that it is today.

Originally a monastery, the building was practically a ruin in Tudor times when it was first owned by the Russell family under the will of Henry VIII. Previously it had remained unoccupied for many years, the Abbot having been hanged for treason at the time of the king's marriage with Anne Boleyn. Five earls later, the owner of Woburn Abbey became the first Duke of Bedford, and successive Dukes have improved and extended the property, the fifth Duke adding the south wing, the Chinese dairy and the orangery.

The furnishings and ornaments gathered over 300 years, the fine portraits and wonderfully painted ceilings all bear witness to an historic heritage.

The grace and charm of the Blue Drawing Room; Queen Victoria's dressing room hung with Dutch and Flemish paintings; the marvellous displays of exquisite Sèvres china and English Stourbridge coloured glass—there was so much to capture my lingering attention as I wandered through the Abbey. But it was the wealth of golden treasure in the centre of the table in the State Dining Room—two equestrian figures flanking the massive Ascot Gold Cup of 1845—that particularly held my eye; for this was to be the setting for my flower arrangement. And since such magnificence could not be rivalled, I decided to pay it homage with low-placed flowers entwined among the gold.

As I set about my design, the Duke and Duchess were both there to greet me. "Are you sure you have everything you need?" the Duke wanted to know. And the Duchess added: "I do hope you enjoy yourself here." Mingled with the beauty of their home, their kindness, courtesy and gaiety of spirit made my visit to Woburn Abbey a truly memorable occasion.

Woburn Abbey: — Woburn Abbey stands in the village of Woburn, Bedfordshire, on the A50 from Dunstable.

LEFT: *The superb Canaletto room at Woburn has the largest collection of the works of this famous Venetian artist in private hands. He made his name in 17th century Venice, painting delightful views of his city, many of which hang here. I made a mass arrangement on the side table, with cerise carnations flowing down one side, and pale green hydrangeas and pink anthuriums on the other.*

Woburn Abbey

ABOVE: *A closer view of the magnificent 1846 Ascot Gold Cup centrepiece, which dominates the dining table. It is flanked by two silver gilt equestrian figures, which came from the breakfast table of the French King Louis XV. With so much silver, gold and glittering glass as a background, the most effective table decoration was one of pink and cerise carnations falling in a swerving line down the length of the table.*

LEFT: *The gilded and decorated ceilings in this, the State Dining Room, should not be missed, and neither should the finely carved George II giltwood console tables on which the gold plate stands. The dinner service on the table is Sèvres, and was made about 1770. The beautiful glassware is English Stourbridge. You may see here, amongst many others, portraits of Charles I and his Queen, Henrietta Maria.*

LEFT: *The Yellow Drawing Room was decorated by the 4th Duke in 1760, and the beautiful ceilings are very much in the French taste of that period. This is the room used by Prince Albert as his sitting room when he stayed here with Queen Victoria in 1841. The portrait above the flowers is of Anne, sister of William, Lord Russell, with an Australian cockatoo—and was painted 150 years before Australia was discovered! The mauve michaelmas daisies and yellow chrysanthemums were picked from the garden.*

RIGHT: *To provide a note of simplicity amongst so much elegance, amongst all the carved wood, the flowered wallpaper, rich furniture and gilt bookbindings, I placed a tall, lichen covered twig with five anthuriums in an antique silver inkstand, and stood it on a beautiful 18th century writing table, made by Montigny. The simple, almost Japanese effect, provided a most marked contrast to the background.*

LEFT: *These clusters of crimson rhododendrons were casually grouped in this elegant marble container. The piece was stood on an 18th century French escritoire, which has a military portrait behind it. The crimson flowers toned beautifully with the colours of the tunic and the background of the painting. Rhododendrons make a very long lasting decoration, particularly if the blooms are picked before they are fully opened.*

LEFT: *Around the walls in the Blue Drawing Room are numerous water colour miniatures, most of which portray members of the Russell family. There are also pictures by Jan Assely (1610–1660), and on either side of the mantelpiece hang 'The Storm' and 'The Sunset' by Joseph Vernet (1714–1789). The magnificent black and gold furniture is French 18th century, which was complemented by the arrangement of pink and crimson chrysanthemums and green amaranthus.*

RIGHT: *This arrangement of simple, pastel coloured shrub roses in an ormolu trimmed Sèvres plate stands on an early period French table. The effect, particularly against the heavy silk wallpaper, is rather like a detail from an idyllic painting by the 18th century French painter, Fragonard. The roses seem to strike a note of formal 18th century gaiety.*

RIGHT: *Detail of the West Front.*

Sutton Place

Not everyone is privileged to see ghosts. For those who are, Sutton Place, near Guildford, Surrey, surely promises a likely haunting ground.

It was in this house, as a guest of its original owner, Sir Richard Weston, that Henry VIII first met his second wife, the ill-fated Anne Boleyn, mother of Queen Elizabeth I. Here, too, was born Sir Richard's son, Francis, whose love for Anne—he was just twenty-one when she became a reluctant royal bride and dubbed him Knight of the Bath at her coronation—later cost him his life on Tower Hill.

But if those two young lovers re-visit the scene of their blighted romance—if Sir Richard, once a favourite at Henry's court, returns to pace the Long Gallery, cursing his friendship with the jealous king as he continues to mourn his son's death—Mr Paul Getty, who purchased Sutton Place from the Duke of Sutherland, seems undisturbed by any such emanations from the historic past.

Perhaps he is not one of those who is aware of the presence of ghosts—if ghosts there be; or perhaps he is more concerned with the twentieth century and the modern visitors he welcomes to the splendours of his English home on those occasions when he opens it to the public for charity.

In any case, we should be grateful to this distinguished American for rescuing Sutton Place from the financial difficulties encountered by so many of our stately homes today, and for restoring and preserving its delights for all to enjoy and admire. He is also maintaining a tradition unbroken for 440 years, because Sutton Place was one of the earliest English manor houses to be built, without fortification, purely as a private dwelling. Since its completion in 1526 it was the home of the Weston family until the beginning of this century and has remained almost unchanged in appearance down to the present day.

Inside the house, the same Brussels tapestries that decorated the walls in Tudor times are still to be seen in the magnificent Long Gallery and Dining Room. Highlighting the Great Hall are no less than 92 of the original latticed bay windows adorned with painted glass shields. Among the arms and devices depicted are those of Henry VIII and Catherine of Aragon, the badge and crown of Jane Seymour, the arms of Philip of Spain and Mary Tudor and a portrait of Charles II. In addition, furnishings and paintings of many different periods and countries make it a collector's paradise.

Outside, Mr Getty's love of plants and flowers is much in evidence. Beautifully tended, about 28 acres of pleasure grounds are in the charge of Mr Newman, the head gardener, who told me that his employer takes a keen interest in the greenhouses. I found Mr Getty a most charming and helpful host and had a wonderful variety of cut flowers to choose from for my arrangements. I like to think that the result might have pleased Anne Boleyn if her ghost happened to be hovering near.

Sutton Place:— 2¼ miles north-east of Guildford, Surrey.

LEFT: *This magnificent still life painting by A. de Connick hangs in the Entrance Hall above a Spanish oak table, on which I arranged white spiraea, yellow daffodils and yellow and bronze tulips, held by wire netting in a Spanish brass container. See how the colours of the flowers I have chosen match those of the painting.*

Sutton Place

ABOVE: *Thanks to Mr Getty's head gardener, Mr Newman, I had plenty of cut flowers to choose from—all from the greenhouses and gardens of the estate. Massed quantities of flowers in this beautiful urn were set at the top of the staircase leading to the Long Gallery. This arrangement lent a festive note to the party that was later held here.*

ABOVE: *The two recesses in the Long Gallery were filled with pink, red and white summer flowers, and a posy of pink sweet peas placed on the tables. The famous Long Gallery is one hundred and sixty-five feet in length, and dates from the original 16th century house. The Brussels tapestries which line the walls have also been here since the house was built.*

ABOVE: *Another view of the Long Gallery, always a feature of Tudor houses, designed so that the ladies of the house could take gentle exercise in bad weather, and to display the owner's paintings and statuary. A magnificent 10th century German walnut sideboard can be seen on the right of my picture. I enjoyed making this colourful arrangement and placing such bright colours in this airy, sunlit room.*

ABOVE: *One of the many treasures to be found in Sutton Place is this painting by Rubens of Diana and her Nymphs, and it hangs in the Tudor Great Hall. I made a long, low arrangement of garden flowers to stand on the table, the predominant yellows catching the warm tints of the picture. The oak panelling is also Tudor, and dates from the building of the house.*

LEFT: *I placed this huge and magnificent Chinese bowl, filled with coleus, cineraria and* begonia rex *plants in this sunny spot, by one of the mullioned windows. The staircase that leads up to the Long Gallery is just out of the picture. Many indoor plants are displayed in the house. The display is changed every two weeks by the head gardener, who produces magnificent begonias and orchids in the greenhouses.*

RIGHT: *Massed carnations, giving a very colourful effect, in the balcony of the Great Hall. Another feature of this room is the carved Tudor fireplace, decorated with the pomegranate emblem of the luckless Catherine of Aragon, who married first Prince Arthur, eldest son of Henry VII and, when widowed, Henry VIII, who later divorced her.*

RIGHT: *One of the many statues in the grounds.*

Penshurst Place

The great Gothic country home of Lord and Lady De L'Isle, near Tonbridge in Kent, dates back to mediaeval times. Penshurst Place, named after its village, began as a manor house built in the 14th century for Sir John de Pulteney, a prosperous wool merchant who was four times Lord Mayor of London; and the original stone house with its massive oak door and cathedral-like porch is still part of the building that you see today. Later owned by a succession of royal dukes, it contains within its ancient walls the huge Baron's Hall with a central hearth and lofty, timbered roof. Suspended from the beams are ten curious, life-size carved wooden figures which are more than 600 years old. Fascinating, too, is the curving stone staircase leading up to the Solar—once a retreat for mediaeval ladies from the noise and turmoil below. For in those days the hall was a communal living room, used for dining and wining as well as for receiving guests, and there was a constant coming and going of servants waiting on their lords and masters.

For nearly 450 years, now, Penshurst Place has belonged to members of the Sidney family. Early in the 16th century, King Edward VI presented it to his Chamberlain, Sir William Sidney, an ancestor of the present owner. More than forty family portraits, covering twelve generations down to Victorian times, can be seen in the Long Gallery and the State Rooms. Among these are several of the famous Elizabethan poet, Sir Philip Sidney, Sir William's eldest grandson who was killed in battle in Holland only four months after his father's death. His brother Robert then inherited the house which, by this time, had been considerably extended. But although many further alterations and additions have been made to the building by succeeding generations, the style of the original architecture has always been faithfully maintained.

Lord De L'Isle, V.C., created a Viscount in 1956, succeeded to the title first conferred on his great-grandfather by Queen Victoria. He came into his inheritance as owner of Penshurst Place in 1945 and lives there with his wife and family in private apartments.

In the gardens, which his grandfather, Lord de L'Isle and Dudley, restored in the last century to much of their early formal charm, I found not only an abundance of beauty and colour in the herbacious borders but a wonderful variety of flowering shrubs and the rich, wine-red foliage of maple trees. To complement the ancient stone interior of the mediaeval part of the house, I decided on a colour-scheme of wine, mauve and purple with a contrast of white—only to discover that flowers had already been picked for me by the head gardener, in shades of yellow, pink, cream and peach.

His flowers—dahlias, roses and hydrangeas—were lovely. But I still long to see the effect of my own idea. One day, perhaps, I shall have the opportunity of visiting Penshurst Place again, and trying it out.

Penshurst Place:— The house is in Penshurst village, on the B2176, near Sevenoaks and Westerham, Kent.

RIGHT: *In the Queen Elizabeth Room, hydrangeas are piled high on one of a pair of gilt candlesticks, which stands near the great carving over the 16th century fireplace. Both this state room, and the next, the Tapestry Room, contain pictures, hangings and furniture of the 17th and 18th centuries. The beautiful 17th century French twenty-four light chandelier is of gilt wood with crystal pendants, and is surmounted by a crown.*

LEFT: *The portraits which hang on the oak panelling of the famous 16th century Long Gallery, are arranged to illustrate the history of the house and the family during the first two centuries following the grant of Penshurst to Sir William Sydney (1482–1554). This arrangement of peach, pink and yellow dahlias was made to go on one of a pair of 18th century German carved gilt commodes.*

RIGHT: *The bank of hydrangeas which I placed on a window ledge of the turreted staircase, gives muted colour to the ancient stonework of this mediaeval part of the house. While I was working here, I was always conscious of a feeling of gratitude that none of the owners of Penshurst was wealthy enough to pull down this Manor House and build a Palladian villa instead of this glorious 14th century home.*

ABOVE: *The long and sunlit room, seen through the stone archway, is the Nether Gallery. White and yellow chrysanthemums were grouped below the portrait. This gallery, together with the Long Gallery, displays a wonderful collection of paintings illustrating the family history back from the present day to Sir William Sidney. All this time the estate has been cherished by the same family.*

RIGHT: *In the Solar I massed red roses in silver containers. The colouring of the roses was strong enough to stand out against the rich background. In this room the visitor can see a set of twelve 18th century upholstered mahogany chairs covered in red damask, the blue velvet stool used by Queen Victoria at her coronation, and a beautiful Italian arch-lute of the 16th century.*

Cliveden

The Saxon meaning of the place-name Cliveden (pronounced without the middle 'e') is 'Valley among the cliffs'. It describes the site, near Maidenhead in Buckinghamshire, of the original house first built for the Duke of Buckingham towards the end of the 17th century. In the following century, some forty years after its completion, Cliveden became the home of Frederick, Prince of Wales, the son of George II and father of George III who lived there until his death in 1751.

Almost exactly a century later the house was destroyed by fire and rebuilt in its present form by the Victorian architect Sir Charles Barry. Its next owner was the Duke of Westminster from whom it was purchased, in 1893, by the first Viscount Astor, and Cliveden has remained the home of the Astor family ever since.

Made over to the National Trust in 1942, it was the residence of the third Viscount Astor and his wife. His American-born mother, the late Nancy, Lady Astor, famous for her dynamic and witty personality, was the first woman Member of Parliament to take her seat in the British House of Commons.

The late Lord Astor's beautiful wife—the dowager Lady Astor—loves to see the house full of flowers, and my Christmas-time visit to Cliveden was specially memorable for her glorious displays of poinsettias, begonias and cyclamen from the hot-houses in the grounds.

Some years previously, when I had visited the house in the spring, the rooms had been decorated with arum lilies and masses of sweet-smelling lilac. On both occasions the same head gardener was in charge of the arrangements—Mr Copcutt, who has been at Cliveden for more than thirty years.

The third Lord Astor was a keen gardener and introduced a number of new flowering shrubs to enhance the beauty of extensive formal gardens for which this stately home is so renowned. Perhaps its most striking feature is the great ornamental pool in front of the house, which is notable for a central group of figures 'floating' on a giant cockleshell. This is the work of the well-known American sculptor, Thomas Story, who designed it from Italian marble shipped from Sienna.

From Italy, too, has come the imposing balustrade standing at the head of the parterre just below the terrace. The graceful chapel is also in Italian style. There are many treasures inside the house, including the fabulous Orkney Tapestries in the Hall.

Cliveden was a wedding present from the first Lord Astor to his son in 1906. Now, sixty years on, his descendents are grateful to the National Trust for making it possible for them to maintain their inheritance as a family home while sharing its beauties with the rest of us.

I shall not forget the warm welcome I was given by my charming hostess—which included, on that frosty winter's day, a glass of rum punch by a glowing log fire when my work was done.

LEFT: *A mass of scarlet flowers stands in front of a portrait of George Villiers, 2nd Duke of Buckingham. Buckingham built the original Cliveden, of which only the huge terraces are left. He eloped with Lady Shrewsbury and the lovers lived there until Buckingham died in 1668. The house lasted, with various changes, until 1795, when it was almost completely destroyed by fire.*

Cliveden: — Cliveden, near Maidenhead, Berkshire, is two miles north of Taplow on the Hedsor road (B476).

LEFT: *Red poinsettias formed the centrepiece of the Christmas dining table decorations. They are the Ecke variety, and were grown on the estate by Mr Copcutt, who has been head gardener to the Astors for more than thirty years. The panelling in the Dining Room came from a house lent by Louis XV to Madame de Pompadour. The furniture is also French.*

RIGHT: *A forty year old orange tree, brought in from the greenhouse and placed in the Hall, is almost a traditional part of Christmas at Cliveden. Standing before the windows, which command a magnificent view of the grounds and the Thames Valley, the green leaves and the glowing fruit make a very pleasant decoration.*

RIGHT: *In the Library, Delft urns were filled with white cyclamen grown from seed. The American type of white spray chrysanthemums were set in fine white china on the mantelpiece. Reynold's portrait of Miss Mary Horneck hangs over the Empire style fireplace. The panelling is a copy of English late 17th century style.*

Cliveden

LEFT: *The Christmas tree at the far end of the Hall was sixteen feet high, and painted white with tinsel and glass baubles as decorations. The base is usually surrounded with Christmas presents. The Hall was redesigned by J. L. Pearson, who was the architect of Truro Cathedral and who altered the existing work of Sir Claude Barry, the designer of the Houses of Parliament.*

RIGHT: *Silvered foliage interspersed with red poinsettias were placed on an oak table in the Hall. The tapestries behind are known as the Orkney set. The Duke of Marlborough presented them to the first Earl of Orkney, who served in the war of the Spanish Succession, and was the first British Field Marshal. They were hung at Cliveden, but disappeared after a fire. The were later found in Paris by the first Viscount Astor, and re-hung.*

RIGHT: *Huge bowls of begonias were placed on tables throughout the house. The bowl shown here was near the famous 16th century French fireplace, which is decorated with the salamander device of François I. The portrait, by Sargent, is of Nancy, Lady Astor. Portraits by Lely and Reynolds also hang in the Hall.*

A large bowl of cut poinsettias and bowls of cyclamen form part of the Christmas decorations in the Large Library. The poinsettias in the corner make an agreeable contrast between the old books with their splendid bindings and the cool and elegant panelling. The portrait over the fireplace is of Mrs Chaplin by Romney.

RIGHT: *The magnificent Dining Room is one of the most remarkable rooms in Cliveden. The splendid Louis XV wainscoting, taken en masse from the Château d'Asnières, has painted canvas panels in each corner. The furniture is also Louis XV. Red poinsettias were used as a centrepiece and also placed either side of the bust of la Marquise de Querylas by Rude, on the mantelpiece.*

Beaulieu

It seems a far cry from the first days of motoring to the last days of the Cistercian monks at Beaulieu Abbey 350 years ago. But Lord Montagu, whose ancestral home in Hampshire was once part of the Abbey—founded by King John in 1204—manages to combine most effectively his world-famous Motor Museum with a proper pride in Beaulieu's ancient history. He has recently replanted the old vineyard with grape vines, and Beaulieu wine is now served to visitors in the public restaurant and cafeteria, housed in one of the original Abbey buildings. The restaurant, with its stone walls and 13th century beamed roof restored in 1909, was formerly a lay brothers' dormitory, and the cafeteria below has been converted from the cellars where the monks stored their own home-made wine.

Beaulieu—Beautiful Place—certainly deserves its name, given at a time when the French language, introduced into the English Court by the Norman conquerors and the first of the Plantagenet kings, was also the natural tongue of the Cistercian religious order, which stemmed from France. Designed to be in keeping with the part Norman, part early English Gothic architectural style of what remains of the Abbey, Lord Montagu's house is set by the upper tidal waters of Beaulieu River and is gloriously surrounded by vast gardens, woodlands and lakes.

During the dissolution of the monastries under King Henry VIII, Beaulieu first became privately owned in 1528 when the Manor House and Abbey were purchased by Thomas Wriothesley, later first Earl of Southampton, whose task it was to destroy the church and most of the Abbey buildings. But some of the latter were left intact, including the Great Gate House, used as a guest house by the monks, which now forms part of Palace House where the present owner lives.

It was through his marriage to Thomas Wriothesley's great-great-granddaughter that Ralph Montagu, third Baron Montagu of Boughton, came into possession of Beaulieu. He was made the first Duke of Montagu by Queen Anne in 1705. Nearly 150 years later, Beaulieu was left to the fifth Duke of Buccleuch who, in turn, gave it as a wedding present to his son, Lord Henry Scott, who was later created the first Baron Montagu of Beaulieu. And it was the baron's grandson who welcomed me to his home and told me: "Please do just as you like with your flowers."

Apart from the additions and alterations carried out by his ancestors, Lord Montagu has made a number of improvements of his own to the residence and grounds, and taken great pleasure in his cherished inheritance. Exploring the old part of Palace House, I discovered some fascinating relics from the days of the monks. Amongst these is a 700-year-old carved oak cupboard, believed to have been the Abbot's bread cabinet, and a secret stone staircase winding up to the roof, which was the only way up to the nursery until towards the end of the century.

Beaulieu: — Beaulieu, Hampshire, is near Lymington, Lyndhurst and Southampton.

LEFT: *Variegated camellia leaves, tall gladioli and old man's beard (wild clematis) give height and width to this design. Yellow and bronze chrysanthemums fill in the outline, and the arrangement is held in an antique Spanish container. The orange-red curtains make a most effective background. The Picture Gallery contains paintings that record the history of the Abbey from the Reformation down to the present day.*

73

Beaulieu

RIGHT: *The Dining Hall is part of the Great Gatehouse of the Abbey. The ceiling vaulting is 13th century, and gives the room its mediaeval character. The mighty elm table, the pointed chairs with coats of arms painted on their backs, the pewter plates and the heavy dressers all add to the general effect.*

BELOW: *This table centrepiece was a dry arrangement of grasses, achillia, various seedheads and physalis, with gourds and artichoke heads as a centre. I fixed the stems of the material in putty stuck on the bark base. The elm table, which seems so much in keeping with this mediaeval room, came from the Servants' Hall of one of the other Montagu family properties.*

ABOVE: *This arrangement was placed in one of the pewter food warmers described below. Scarlet nerines and the brilliantly coloured anemones added interest to the grouping of the fruit, mushrooms, tomatoes, nuts and leaves. The whole design makes a very vivid and sparkling contrast to the muted background colours and it seems to light up this corner of the room.*

LEFT: *The massive, heavily carved sideboard holds a collection of 18th century pewter plates and water heated serving dishes. The latter were kept hot with boiling water. The pictures in their gold frames catch the soft glow of the polished wood and pewter, and form a subdued background to the arrangement.*

ABOVE: *One of the mellow stone windows made an ideal background for this dramatic arrangement of the stalks of Indian millet and corncobs. Pale green dried bamboo leaves and brown preserved fatzia leaves are grouped round the base. The oldest part of Beaulieu was once part of the Great Gatehouse of the Abbey, and much of the original 13th century work is preserved in the present house.*

LEFT: *These lilies, placed in front of a plaque of the Virgin and Child, drew attention to the ancient piscina in which I stood them. The piscina, which is a small basin used for washing the sacramental vessels in some churches, suggests that this room was once the chapel built above the Great Gatehouse. Lord Montagu now uses it as his private dining room.*

RIGHT: *The dry blue hydrangeas and statice, interspersed with pampas grass, forms this arrangement on a table in the Drawing Room, which has many distinctive features. The gothic fireplace is very fine and so are the vaulted ceilings and stone arches. Since the Reformation the house has undergone many changes, but many traces of its ecclesiastical origins are still noticeable.*

Harewood House

Designed by Adam, decorated by Rose, Zucchi and Kaufmann, furnished by Chippendale, with landscape by Capability Brown .... With such a galaxy of star talent among its 18th century creators, it is hardly surprising that Harewood House, in Yorkshire, should be the criterion of elegance, both inside and out. Yet one is surprised by the sheer perfection of this stately home that has scarcely changed since it was first built for Edwin Lascelles, Lord Harewood, when he inherited a West Indian sugar fortune two hundred years ago.

In a country village midway between Leeds and Harrogate, Harewood House was, until recently, the home of Her Royal Highness the late Princess Royal, wife of the sixth Earl of Harewood and sister of King George VI. Now it is owned by her son and daughter-in-law, the seventh Earl and his Countess, both renowned music-lovers and, like Princess Mary, keen and knowledgeable horticulturists.

Harewood's picturesque timbered setting and ornamental lake in the grounds are typical of Brown's handiwork, and this truly gracious home houses the celebrated Harewood collection of Chinese porcelain in the Gallery where many beautiful paintings are also displayed. Among these are family portraits by such famous painters as Reynolds, Gainsborough, Romney and Hoppner. The visitor's gaze falls, too, in other rooms, on the works of such Italian Old Masters as Titian, Tintoretto and Veronese whose illustrious names have illuminated history.

The famous Gallery, which is 24 feet wide and nearly 80 feet long, is one of Robert Adam's most spectacular achievements. He also designed the carpets in keeping with the ceiling patterns. The unique fringed window pelmets, which are carved in wood to resemble richly draped taffetas, were made in Chippendale's workshops.

Everywhere it is the exquisite artistry, fine craftsmanship and meticulous attention to detail that both astonishes and delights the eye. All is superbly wrought with the care and skill that is seldom, if ever, found in the houses of modern times. And still (in 1966) proudly presiding here is Mr Blades, the butler who devotedly served the Princess Royal for more than thirty years.

In addition to the extensive gardens that surround it, Harewood House has its own 1,500-acre home farm with 1,000 acres of forest, and is the centre of a large agricultural estate of twenty other farms all making a valuable contribution to Britain's agricultural industry.

But it is as one of the great treasure houses of the north that this wonderful home deserves to be visited—not just once but again and again. The visitor will soon realize that it represents more than the best that money can buy. Unchanged in a changing world, it stands today as a heart-lifting reminder of the beauty and serenity that England still has to offer.

Harewood House: — Harewood village, Yorkshire, is on the A61 between Leeds and Harrogate.

LEFT: *This beautiful gilded mirror reflects the Reynolds painting of the elegant Countess of Harrington, one of the many famous works that hang in the Gallery. There is so much gilding blazing from the picture frames, from the surrounds of the mirrors, and from the carved chairs, that the simple arrangement of palm, phlox and* begonia rex *refreshes the passing eye, without detracting from the elegance of this room.*

ABOVE: *Two gilt console tables with inlaid marble tops stand either side of the white and green marble fireplace in the Green Drawing Room. I used one of them for this harmonising arrangement of auratum lilies, yellow and white spray chrysanthemums, yellow gladioli, green onion heads and hosta leaves. The whole effect had to be kept low to avoid obscuring the portrait behind.*

LEFT: *The green and white marble fireplace in the Green Drawing Room was the inspiration for the colour scheme of my arrangement. Green, white and yellow plant material follows the lines of the sofa table in front of the fire. The outline was made of fine foliage and yellow gladioli, and the centre marked by auratum lilies. Yellow and white chrysanthemums, green and white tradescantia and* Hosta marginata *leaves and green allium heads were used to fill in the design.*

83

Harewood House

LEFT: *The Gallery at Harewood is one of Adam's greatest and most elegant creations. Every detail, from the carved* trompe l'œil *Chippendale curtain draperies over the windows, to the designs in the gilded mirror uprights, reflects his genius for decoration. This large arrangement in pink, crimson and white was placed on one of the console tables. Summer jasmine flows down one side, and onopordon thistle on the other.*

BELOW: *Three beautiful yellow roses are placed in the mouth of this exquisite vase from the famous Harewood collection. Known as a K'anh Hsi vase, it was made in China between 1662 and 1795, and shipped to France, where the Louis XV ormolu mounting was added to it. A flourishing trade in objets d'art then existed between China and the West.*

ABOVE: *The Music Room is yet another example of Adam's genius. The carpet was designed by him to reflect the pattern on the ceiling as were the gilt chairs, upholstered with pink, flowery Beauvais tapestry. Below the striking Sèvres clock which once belonged to Marie Antoinette, I placed pink larkspur, crimson centred* Pandorea jasminoides *and crimson godetia.*

Harewood House

LEFT: *Crumpled wire held this large, colourful arrangement in the fireplace of the Rose Drawing Room. Pink gladioli, white arum lilies, pink larkspur, crimson godetias and grey thistles are blended to make an interesting and eyecatching appearance and to highlight the classical fire grate and fender.*

RIGHT: *This chimneypiece by Sir Claude Berry is a later addition to the Adam Gallery. Some idea of the scale of the paintings and the height of the mantelpiece may be gained from the fact that the arrangement is ten feet high from the floor to the top of the palm. Pot plants were grouped in the huge* famille rose *container, placed on a white and gold stool.*

LEFT: *The elegant, ormolu-trimmed wine cooler made a superb container for my arrangement. The lid, which is four feet across, was half opened, and the cooler filled with green foliage, yellow cannas and zinnias, with some white candidum lilies. The Dining Room is noted for its display of gold-rimmed Venetian glass, and also for the portrait of the Princess Royal by Sir Oswald Birley.*

Chatsworth House

Known as the Palace of the Peak, Chatsworth House is the Derbyshire home of the Dukes of Devonshire and has belonged to the Cavendish family since the middle of the 16th century. Apart from the chapel, however, almost nothing of the original Elizabethan Chatsworth now remains. Built for its first owner, Sir William Cavendish, in 1552, it was pulled down some 130 years later by his great-great-grandson, the first Duke of Devonshire, who twice rebuilt it during his lifetime.

Further sweeping changes and improvements were made during the 18th and 19th centuries, and there have been many more since. Owned today by the eleventh Duke, Chatsworth is considered to be one of the finest homes in England.

Outside, in the magnificent gardens and park, there is the cool splashing of fantastic fountains, notably the Emperor fountain, the second largest in the world. Inside, the visitor will find splendour upon splendour—damask and velvet, polished wood and marble, scarlet and gold—as he moves from the great Painted Hall, with its dramatic red-carpeted, gilded stairway, into the State Rooms.

I was curious to know how George II's canopied bed came to be here, and discovered that, as Lord Chamberlain at the time of the king's death, the fourth Duke had acquired it by right. I wondered, too, what had been the original purpose of the Grotto—an elaborately decorated ground-floor room containing a marble fountain with carvings in stone. This, I learned, had been specially built by the first Duke for the lowest flight of his 'new' staircase which he later moved to the Painted Hall.

But there is one mystery at Chatsworth that has remained unsolved for nearly 300 years: a picture by Simon Vouet, *Allegory of Peace*, which hangs over one of the doorways. This is one of a series, painted for Louis XIII of France in the 1620's, and already at Chatsworth in the first Duke's time. But the other paintings in the series are still where they always have been—in the Palace of St Germain. So how did this one become separated from the others? Nobody knows, nor, most probably, ever will know, now.

I was fascinated to find that the time-honoured tradition of flower arranging by the Head Gardener, Mr Bert Link, is still observed in this house, though the Duchess, a keen interior decorator and tremendously interested in flowers, suggests the schemes. There were plants and flowers everywhere, especially in the private appartments; and I specially admired a lovely arrangement of blue delphiniums and cream stock which had been picked from the garden and which the Duchess had placed in a bedroom known as the View Room to welcome an expected guest.

The magnificent view from the windows—a panorama of the Derbyshire hills and the River Derwent that flows past the house —is one of the great beauties of Chatsworth whose grounds, possibly the most famous garden of any stately home, owe much of their effect to the succession of great gardening figures, Capability Brown, Sir Joseph Paxton, and many others.

LEFT: *Large bowls of massed flowers set among candles give a softer look to the immense table in the Dining Room. This whole room, from the sheer size and weight of its furnishings and decorations, gives an impression of luxury. The many Van Dyck pictures, which were painted at the height of the master's career, together with the richly carved gilt tables and fine china from the Devonshire collection, all add to the room's general magnificence.*

Chatsworth: — Chatsworth is near Bakewell, Derbyshire, opposite the village of Edensor on the A623.

ABOVE: *This flower pyramid, containing pink and cerise carnations, repeats the colour scheme of the dining table. Chatsworth has always been famous for its gardens, and all the flowers used have come from the estate. Sir Joseph Paxton, the architect of Crystal Palace, was Head Gardener here, and built the huge greenhouse, now demolished, that was the prototype for the Great Exhibition building.*

LEFT: *The private Dining Room decorated for a Ball to celebrate the coming of age of Lord Hartington, the Duke of Devonshire's eldest son. The gilt epergnes, by Thomire, are filled with mixed pink and cerise geraniums. The folding screen is particularly rich and colourful, and the gilded surrounds to the paintings match the ornamented ceiling and door frames.*

Chatsworth House

LEFT: *The private apartments were redecorated by the present Duchess, and are most charming and habitable rooms. The biggest criticism that has been levelled at Chatsworth is that the State Rooms are not quite as effective as the exterior and the setting of the house, because their main function is as backgrounds to display the magnificent Devonshire treasures. Massed garden flowers were used for the arrangement.*

RIGHT: *The comfortable Blue Drawing Room is part of the private suite of rooms. The gilding over the windows and the ornamental ceiling do not overawe here, and the visitor carries away an impression of cheerful comfort. The rooms are kept filled with flowers by Mr Link, the Head Gardener, and are arranged with that studied carelessness that only the expert can achieve.*

LEFT: *Massed pansies, arranged on a mound of wet sand, and backed by a gold plate stand. Chatsworth is still very much a family home, and the works of art, rich decoration and magnificient furniture are no more than a background in the private rooms to the everyday way of life of the family when it is in residence. This arrangement is in the private Dining Room.*

LEFT: *A mixed bouquet of herbaceous flowers, contained in a bronze urn. The gay colours and multiplicity of shapes bring an informal note to the dignified windows and tall rooms. The twisted iron supports that hold up these flowers were designed and manufactured in the estate workshops.*

RIGHT: *Henry VIII stares arrogantly down from his heavily gilded frame in this portrait, after Holbein, by Hans Eworth. The simplicity of this free-flowing arrangement of orchids (Calanthe regneiri) contrasts vividly with the ornate frame and carved table. The flowers are set in a silver-gilt 18th century wine-cooler, made by David Tanquerary. The delicate colours of the flowers reflect the golden tones that prevail in this setting.*

LEFT: *Beautifully cultivated fuchsias and other flowering plants are massed in the private corridors. I was fortunate to be welcomed into the family portion of the house and allowed to range at will with my photographer. The state apartments must be amongst the most photographed sets of rooms in Britain, and I was happy that I was able to capture some of the less familiar aspects of Chatsworth.*

Wakehurst Place

A paradise both for garden-lovers and serious students of plant-life—this is what Wakehurst Place, in Sussex, soon to be known as 'Kew in the country', is about to become. For its last private owner, the late Sir Henry Price, left it to the National Trust, and it is now leased to the Royal Botanical Gardens whose directors are planning to open it to the public in 1966.

Even so, Wakehurst remains the home that it always has been since the great quadrangular house was first built in Elizabethan times. Lady Price, Sir Henry's widow, still lives there and loves to design her own flower arrangements from the wealth of wonderful material in the gardens and grounds.

Wakehurst's first owner was Sir Edward Culpepper, in 1690, and there have been Culpeppers in Sussex ever since, down to the present day. I like to think that the famous 17th century herbalist, Nicholas Culpepper, a younger kinsman of Sir Edward, often came here to seek the plants he needed for his healing potions. I like to think, too, that he would be glad to know that the glories of Wakehurst have been preserved for other garden-lovers like himself to share and enjoy.

On the eastern edge of Worth Forest, the grounds include 500 acres of natural woodland, planted with oaks, beeches, limes, horse-chestnuts, maples and many other fine trees, where avenues of rhododendrons, rock ravines and rivulets are sudden, delightful surprises. Another hundred acres of cultivated gardens are embroidered with shrubberies and ponds and laced with romantic arbours and shady walks.

This is the fascinating setting for a house which, in spite of changes made by its various owners at different times, has largely retained its architectural style of nearly four centuries ago. About one hundred years after it was built, one side of the quadrangle was removed, and the projections of the east and west wings were shortened from eighty-seven to twenty-four feet in the middle of the last century. The chapel was added by the Marchioness of Downshire, who lined the interior with oak panelling taken from the drawing room on the first floor, and part of the inside of the house has since been modernised.

Although these changes have not robbed the building of its historic interest, it will nevertheless be mainly for the sake of the gardens that thousands will soon find their way to Wakehurst Place, in the little Sussex village of Ardingly.

Visit it, and you will find yourself in another world—a world in which Nature combined with artistry has produced a very heaven-on-earth that is full of bird-song in springtime and heady with the scent of flowers all summer long.

I was not looking for herbs when I wandered enchanted here. But the atmosphere evoked them like poetry in my mind ... rosemary, majoram, bergamot ... as I walked where Nicholas Culpepper must surely have walked long, long ago.

Wakehurst Place: — Five miles north of Haywards Heath, Sussex.

LEFT: *This urn of mauve and pink flowers was placed in the panelled Dining Room. Tall sprays of* Galega officinalis *and purple lythrum gave the height to the design, and defoliated lime sprays its width. Pink Queen Elizabeth roses marked the centre and the design was filled in with mauve erigeron, rosy pink* Sedum spectabile *and astrantia flowers.*

ABOVE RIGHT: *The abundance of fine plant material enabled me to make this colourful design without using any flowers. Lime green leaves are placed down one side and maroon the other, with stems of variegated Spanish chestnut high in the centre, and shiny* Magnolia grandiflora *leaves as the central interest. Green-brown magnolia seedpods made a contrast in shapes.*

RIGHT: *This elegant writing desk, set in one of the Drawing Room windows, made an excellent pedestal for the arrangement. Peach coloured eremurus, with sprays of stripped lime are used as a background for yellow achillia and pink pyrethrums. The stems were held in the glass vase by concealed wire netting. Eremurus, although a perennial plant, is often called foxtail lily.*

Wakehurst Place

ABOVE: *A view of the Jacobean house across one of the lakes. Beautiful groups of trees grow round the lakes, in which may be seen many fine varieties of water plants. Lakes and ponds have always been associated from the earliest times with large houses. They were first used for keeping fish for household use and became an ornamental feature of the landscape later.*

RIGHT: *A feature of the grounds at Wakehurst are the many sundials carefully placed to form focal points for the vistas. They all provide a delightful contrast between weathered stone, green lawns and blooming flowers. The visitor may well agree with the old tag, to be found on one of them, Et in Arcadia ego. Truly, the gardens here form an idyllic setting for the house.*

RIGHT: *A massive bowl of mixed roses placed in the window of the Drawing Room. Most of the house is Elizabethan, and the warm stone of the walls suits the lovely setting to perfection. The mullioned windows look out across the lawns and the ornamental waters to the wooded grounds extending along the eastern edge of the Worth Forest.*

BOTTOM LEFT: *Massed rhododendrons, particularly Pink Pearl, are found in many places in the grounds, which are now under the care of the Royal Botanical Gardens, who are caring for the interesting and rare plants that are grown here and frequently introducing new varieties.*

BOTTOM RIGHT: *A fine euphorbia, growing beside the neatly trimmed lawns. Wakehurst has always had connections with botany. A relation of the first owner, Sir Edward Culpepper, was a well-known botanist in the 16th century, and it may be that he gained some of his knowledge and interest in plants from Wakehurst's famous gardens.*

Syon House

The 16th century London home of the Duke and Duchess of Northumberland is modestly named; for the great, quadrangular stone edifice of Syon, with its crenellated turrets and walls, is a castle rather than a house. Built in 1547 on the site of an abandoned monastry, it stands by the Thames at Twickenham and has belonged to the Percy family for more than 350 years.

Its riverside setting and water-meadows inspired Canaletto, the famous Italian artist, to make a painting of Syon House when he visited London in the middle of the 18th century. Ten years later, in 1762, Hugh Percy, first of the ducal line re-created by King George III, engaged two of the most celebrated craftsmen of the time—architect and designer Robert Adam and landscape gardener Lancelot (Capability) Brown—to reconstruct the whole of the interior of the building and the layout of the surrounding gardens and park. It is largely the work of these two men that made Syon, like so many of Britain's stately homes, a lasting monument to their skill and artistry, which has happily survived even the bombs of war.

In the following century a huge glass conservatory, now housing hundreds of rare botanical species and tropical plants, was built in grounds by the third Duke who established what his grandfather had already begun—Syon's reputation for specialist cultivation of plants, shrubs and trees from all over the world.

This tradition has been fostered and maintained by succeeding generations, and the present owner, the tenth Duke, well known for his interest in farming and horticulture, has designated part of the 200-acre park as Britain's Garden Centre, with the conservatory as its hub, to be opened in 1967.

It was at Syon, during Queen Victoria's reign, that clove, vanilla, cocoa and nutmeg plants were brought to perfection. And the Duke told me of future plans for the centre that will include, he hopes, a restaurant, conference hall, reference library, exhibition section, demonstration area and other facilities to cater for hundreds of thousands of visitors each season. For this wonderful scheme is likely to prove an even greater attraction for flower-lovers and plant-growing enthusiasts than the famous show gardens just across the river at Kew.

Meanwhile, the house itself has its own fascination, offering superb examples of Adam interiors. Marble pillars, mosaic floors, ornamented ceilings, gilded statuary . . . here is an intricacy and richness of design which speaks of an age of elegance that will never come again. It was against this background that such visitors as Princess Victoria, Prince Talleyrand, the Duke of Wellington and many other distinguished guests were royally entertained by the third Duke. The sofa they sat on in the Red Drawing Room, the Long Gallery where they paced after dinner, the magnificent Sèvres vase—a gift to their host from King Charles X of France—they admired in the Dining Room are still here, as if waiting expectantly for the crinolined ladies and frock-coated gentlemen to reappear once more.

LEFT: *The Great Hall is one of the five superb rooms designed and decorated by Robert Adam in the Jacobean framework of Syon. The impression the visitor gains is of a vast Roman temple moved bodily to England. Doric columns, marble statues, black and white tiled floors and magnificent stucco work make this a dignified and formal room. A copy of Valadier's Dying Gaul has been surrounded by a group of house plants.*

Syon House: — Syon House is on the north bank of the Thames between Brentford and Isleworth.

ABOVE: *The Long Gallery is perhaps Adam's greatest triumph. Most houses built before the 18th century had one, and it has always been a problem to fit them up for everyday habitation. Adam solved the problem by designing the furniture and the decorations to adapt this room into a drawing room. Red gladioli, pale green hydrangeas and pink belladonna lilies with maroon* Prunus pissardi *to give width, were arranged here on a chimneypiece.*

ABOVE: *This swerved arrangement of red and pink carnations and blue green rhus is held by wire in a cherub container. Much of the impact that the Long Gallery makes on the visitor is directly attributable to the colours that Adam decorated it in—old gold and a beautiful pale green, which contrasts strongly with the bindings of the books which line the walls.*

RIGHT: *In the Red Drawing Room I stood two of these enchanting cone-shaped designs on small tables. A cone of wire netting, filled with moss, has small roses, bunches of berries, grapes and leaves wired and inserted into it. The magnificent carpet, the finest of its kind, and the exquisite ceiling, painted by Angelica Kauffman, are harmonious parts of Adam's conception of what a room should look like.*

104

LEFT AND RIGHT: *Two views of an eight foot high pillar of flowers in the Dining Room. The pale green Love-lies-bleeding* (Amaranthus caudatus) *in the centre helps to lighten the effect of the reds and pinks making up the rest of the arrangement which is contained in two vases, one inside the other. Adam designed this room as a place for the gentlemen to linger over their port and cigars, and, so that no trace of cooking smells or smoke should hang here, he ordered that no curtains or draperies should grace the windows.*

LEFT: *This beautiful, classical white and gold vase is filled with gilded beech leaves, artichokes, fruits and seedheads. It stands on one of the many elegant side tables, the top of which is made of mosaic found in the ancient Baths of Titus in Rome. In 1760, when Adam was asked to design the interior, he had just returned from a tour of Rome, and he was very enthusiastic in adopting a classical style to 18th century requirements.*

RIGHT: *This group stood in the Long Gallery. Yellow gladioli, dahlias, and chrysanthemums formed the outline, and green nicotiana and* Euphorbia wulfenii *filled the centre. Berries, astrantia and autumn foliage complete the arrangement. Some idea of the immense length of this room, 136 feet, may be gained from this, but Adam's work appears to shorten and widen it to habitable proportions.*

L'Envoi

I am sorry that I could not visit many, many more of the wonderful houses with which Britain is so richly endowed. Nowhere else in the world can the visitor find so many noble monuments to a more spacious age—yet this very abundance of historic and impressive buildings brought me many problems. Which to choose, which to leave out: always the most difficult task for any writer on this subject. I finally decided that I would include only those houses which were most familiar to my readers, rather than those famous for some architectural feature, or those with the most historic appeal. Then too I have tried to describe those houses that are still cherished and much loved family homes.

Even within these limitations I have been left wishing that I had had more space to include further examples of these splendid houses which are truly an important part of our heritage. I have, however, included at the end of this book information which will help the reader to discover and visit the many stately homes of Britain.

With many omissions I have included on the following pages a number of flower arrangements that I thought would be particularly apt for various other houses that I have not had the opportunity to visit to arrange the flowers *in situ*. I have carried away an impression of the decor and the shapes of the different rooms, and have then created an arrangement to suit the room. Although flowers bring a feeling of life into any setting, the study and careful assessment of the details that go to make up the background and the framework that your flowers are going to fill is essential. Colour, texture, and the design you want for your flowers must all have a place in your planning if you are to create an arrangement that will have the maximum effect in these lavish settings.

I have also added some advice at the end of this part of the book that will enable you to plan your own arrangements, and will give you a starting point for experimenting with designs that you can create yourself.

Here then is a selection of pictures of well-known houses. Crathes Castle, a house that is clearly marked by the turbulent past, designed as a refuge, and a bastion against the clan skirmishes and cattle raids that characterise Scottish history. Nostell Priory—built in the 18th century, reflecting in its design the very essence of that spacious, cultured and dignified century; Hopetoun House, another Scottish house, but a complete contrast to the warrior-keep that is Crathes, with its beautiful Adam frontages and magnificent art treasures. Saltram, Mereworth, Newby, Burghley, Belvoir Castle, Holkham—all these have played their parts in our history, and all serve as monuments to the creative spirit and loving attention to detail that their builders displayed.

There are many more, but I hope that these examples will show you just what can be done with flowers to bring even more warmth and colour into such superb interiors.

LEFT: *The Great Hall on the first floor of Crathes Castle is an example of domestic comfort placed second to dictates of defence. When Crathes was built, in the 16th century, the prudent landowner protected himself from marauding Highlanders. The narrow stairway, the six foot thick walls and the slit windows, all are marks of Scotland's turbulent past. The horn of tenure granted by Robert Bruce hangs over the mantelpiece in this room.*

Nostell Priory, Wakefield

This house was designed in 1733 by James Paine when he was only nineteen, and was the first Palladian house to be built in the north of England. Although the house was altered by Adam, and many of the rooms redecorated, the dining room, shown opposite, is as Paine designed it. His work on Nostell established him as a successful country house architect.

The original builder, Sir Rowland Win, a descendant of the first Queen Elizabeth's draper, died before the work was completed, and his son entrusted the rest of the work to Adam, who built another wing, and changed some of Paine's interiors. The furniture was mostly built by Chippendale, and many fine paintings, particularly Holbein's portrait of Sir Thomas More and his family, are on view.

I felt that a simple but colourful arrangement of old-fashioned roses would suit the ornate plasterwork and magnificent furniture that is such a feature of this house, and I have illustrated below an arrangement that I thought would be particularly suitable in this gracious, Italian renaissance atmosphere.

The house was presented by Lord St Oswald to the National Trust.

RIGHT: *The Dining Room at Nostell, showing the original Paine plasterwork and designs. Massed roses have been set in the wine coolers, and fruit placed in the candelabra, providing a pleasant splash of colour against the formal glitter of the silver and crystal services set on the table.*

BELOW: *An arrangement of old-fashioned roses, which, I feel, provides a contrasting note of simplicity and life to the very ornate and grandiose surroundings, and which would not compete with the mannered style of the plasterwork and the fireplace. It is always of the utmost importance that the arrangement should be related to the background against which it is to stand.*

Hopetoun House, Nr Edinburgh

This is a magnificent example of the Adam family collaboration. Originally designed by William Adam, it was finished by his two famous sons, John and Robert. It is amongst the finest classical houses in Scotland.

Now the home of the Marquis of Linlithgow, Hopetoun contains very fine pictures and furniture. I noticed particularly the huge *Adoration of the Shepherds* by Rubens, the great Flemish painter-diplomat.

Many of the rooms are decorated with rich and colourful silk brocades, which needed very strong, bold arrangements to have any marked effect. Any pale, small, harmonic decorations would be completely lost in the vast rooms, which are encrusted with rich plasterwork and gilt ornamentation, and lit by crystal chandeliers.

The arrangement in the Red Drawing Room had also to stand out from the Charles II torchères used as a pedestal-stand. It had to compete with the red patterned wallpaper and elaborate gilt picture frame. The design in the Yellow Drawing Room was set against the heavily gilded mirrors and the finest pictures in the Hopetoun collection.

RIGHT: *The Red Drawing Room seemed to me to call for this arrangement of green and yellow garden flowers. The outline was formed by green fern, Molucella laevis (Bells of Ireland), green nicotiana flowers, greeny-yellow gladioli and ivy. Yellow cactus, dahlias, onion heads and berries marked the centre.*

LEFT: *I grouped flame coloured gladioli, bronze dahlias and cream lilies with green leaves to form a low triangular effect, and placed them on a gilt console table in the Yellow Drawing Room. The elaborately carved table and the candle holders beside the mirror dictated the shapes of the arrangement.*

Belvoir Castle, Lincolnshire

The original castle was built for the standard bearer of William the Conqueror. Since then the castle has been rebuilt three times, and the present building was commenced in 1800, and was designed by James Wyatt. After Wyatt's death, a fire in 1816 swept away a large part of his work, and the task of rebuilding and completing the castle was given to a relation of the 5th Duke of Rutland, the Reverend Sir John Thornton.

The exterior of the castle is in the romantic Gothic style, as is the Guard Room and the main staircases and the corridors. The rest of the interior is decorated in a wide variety of styles, ranging from Norman to Chinese, with classical rooms and French rococo—truly a medley, but so grand is the scale of building that none of them seem to be entirely out of place.

BELOW: *This design was made of dry palmetto leaves and blackened wood around a sculptured iron stand. Lotus seed heads and dry proteas formed the centre, and the arrangement matches the ray effect of the sword trophy.*

LEFT: *The Guard Room at Belvoir is a fine example of the Romantic Gothic movement in architecture. Trophies of swords, guns, standards and accoutrements are used to produce the effect of a mediaeval armoury, and to make a grandiose entrance to the Castle.*

Standing outside Saltram, the visitor would never guess that this austere Georgian house, with its unadorned whitewashed walls, conceals a Tudor core. In 1768, the ubiquitous Robert Adam was commissioned to alter and redecorate some of the rooms, and it is his influence that, as usual, predominates and pervades the house.

The Saloon, one of Adam's finest works, is a truly magnificient yet elegant example of his attention to the smallest detail of interior decoration. Every motif, every door handle, reflects Adam's passionate concern to harmonise the effects that go to make up a room into one splendid picture. Even the carpet was designed by him and carefully woven to match the ceiling.

The Parkers, former owners of this lovely estate, were friends of Sir Joshua Reynolds, and they had his help and advice in the selection of the pictures, which include fourteen portraits from the artist's own hand.

All these treasures, and its landscaped grounds, make Saltram a house of great charm and distinction.

ABOVE: *This arrangement of white delphiniums, pink roses, white philadelphus and green leaves, loosely arranged on an ormolu table, would be particularly suitable for the Saloon.*

RIGHT: *A corner of the Adam Saloon. Notice particularly the way in which the carpet mirrors the ceiling decoration. The glittering chandeliers with their thousand of gleaming glass brilliants are also a notable feature.*

Newby Hall, Ripon

Two strong influences are immediately apparent at Newby, and both are from great ages in English country house architecture. The main block was built in the Wren manner, and the wings and sculpture gallery were built by Adam.

William Weddell, who engaged Adam, was a famous collector of classical statuary, and Adam created a splendid gallery for him to display his treasures. Adam also redesigned many of the old rooms making one of them a suitable background to display a magnificent set of Gobelins tapestries.

The gardens, running down to the River Ure, are comparatively modern, but are widely noted for their collection of unusual plants, trees and shrubs. These gardens, rich in botanical interest, provide a worthy setting for the mansion.

BELOW: *This arrangement seemed suitable for the Tapestry Room. Two gilt cherubs support a flowing pattern of freesia, daisies, green leaves and mimosa which would harmonize with the glowing flowers of the Gobelins.*

LEFT: *The Tapestry Room contains some of the exquisite Gobelins tapestries, whose soft colours blend perfectly with the gilt legged chairs and sofas, and the rich patterning of the ceiling.*

Perhaps one of the greatest single influences on English classical architecture was the 16th century Italian architect, Andrea Palladio, who was certainly idolised by Inigo Jones. There was also no doubt that Campbell, who designed Mereworth, was much impressed by Jones. The result of these influences is that this Kentish castle is a copy of Palladio's most famous house, the Villa Rotonda at Vicenza.

Although Mereworth looks like a Roman temple, inside it is a most comfortable and convenient family home. The visitor is first impressed by the huge hall, built under the rotunda, with its beautiful Bagutti stucco work set against the background of the roughened terracotta walls.

The colourful and sumptuous rooms, where not a square inch of undecorated surface can be seen, would almost be too rich if it was not for the perfect taste and proportions they display. Mereworth, then, is a happy blend between the lofty and monumental architectual style of ancient Rome and an English country house.

RIGHT: *I made this very effective dry plant arrangement to complement the stucco work. The scallop shells, beech leaves, poppy seed heads, Australian gum pods, artichokes, dried gourds, lemons, small cones, grasses and artificial grapes are anchored in putty on a slat of wood and painted white.*

RIGHT: *Part of the circular hall that fills the space under the great dome. Bagutti's rich and ornate stucco work and figures contrast most effectively with the plain, slightly roughened terracotta walls.*

Burghley House, Northamptonshire

Burghley is the second of the great houses built by the Cecil family. Theobalds, the other, was exchanged for Hatfield House (p. 30), but Burghley has been a family possession since 1552.

The house has been described as the greatest and the most extensive Elizabethan monument. Although the interior has been altered over the centuries, the exterior has not been changed since the last of Lord Burghley's masons laid down their tools in the 1580's.

The interior is as ornate and imaginative as the outside. Little of the original decorations remain, except in the Great Hall. The 5th Earl, who spent much of his time in Italy, commissioned various artists to fit up and redecorate his home in the classical manner. Perhaps the most splendidly decorated room in any English house is Verrio's Heaven Room. The entire surface of the walls and ceilings is covered with a huge allegorical painting, giving the visitor the impression he has strayed into a temple bursting with mythical gods and goddesses.

ABOVE: *This garland seemed to be an obvious choice for this room. It could be hung round the vast silver wine cooler, and it echoes the garlands that are painted between the columns on the wall.*

LEFT: *The elaborate decoration of Verrio's Heaven Room is surely one of the most ornate pieces of interior decoration ever conceived. The entire mythical pantheon can be seen in characteristic poses, covering the walls and ceilings.*

Holkham is the finest Palladian house in England. The exterior is more imposing than ornamental because the undecorated surfaces give an impression of austerity, relieved only by the columns and the shapes of the roof. The brick used, which is dun coloured, does nothing to alter this impression. Once inside, however, all the austerity of the exterior is forgotten. The builders, Thomas Coke, who later became Earl of Leicester, and William Kent, selected their designs from the works of Palladio, Inigo Jones and Roman models. The result is the crowning point in the development of building in the 18th century.

The entrance Hall, which is a modified copy of a Roman basilica, leads the visitor between lines of huge columns of Derbyshire alabaster to the magnificent Saloon on the first floor. This room, which blazes with colour, contains the best of the many important paintings that hang at Holkham. Resting against the original red Genoa velvet, Van Dykes and Rubens, including the famous *Return from Egypt*, make this room a veritable treasure house of art.

RIGHT: *One of the glories of Holkham is the huge Marble Hall that serves as the entrance. Rising almost to the full height of the house, the great alabaster columns and the ornamented ceiling create an atmosphere of great stateliness.*

BELOW: *A pedestal arrangement seems to me to be the only economic way to decorate the huge Hall. Standing beside the red carpeted stairs, it would contrast admirably with the alabaster podium walls.*

Ways to keep cut flowers alive longer

Arrangements of mixed flowers will last longer if you:

1

Always pick your flowers before they are fully mature.

2

Pick them at night or early in the morning, when transpiration is at its lowest.

3

Split the stem-ends of all leaf-sprays and foliage before submerging them overnight, or for several hours, in a bath of water to which a tablespoonful of sugar has been added.

4

Re-cut the stem-ends of picked flowers and stand them in deep, tepid water overnight, or for several hours, before starting an arrangement.

5

Remove some of the lower leaves from woody stemmed flowers, such as roses, lilac, azalea or viburnum, and split the stem-ends before standing them in deep, tepid water.

6

Put a small amount of tepid water into your vase before starting an arrangement—to prevent the stem-ends from becoming dry; and fill up with more water when the arrangement is completed.

7

Add a tablet of charcoal to the water in the vase to keep it pure and a teaspoonful of sugar, or other preservative such as chrysal, to help keep the flowers fresh.

8

Top up the vase with fresh water every day, or twice a day in warm weather when evaporation is faster.

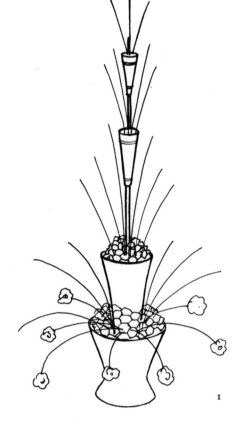

On the opposite page I show the basic build-up of some of the designs featured in the photographs. These techniques can be adapted to make smaller or larger arrangements to suit your choice.

1

Showing the basic structure of the 8ft. high side chimneypiece arrangements seen at Syon House (page 106). Stand one vase inside the other (substitutes could be tins or bowls) inserting metal cones wired to sticks in the top one. Place wire netting in each of the lower vases and make the tall outline of the design by placing fine tall flowers in the top cone working down to the lowest vase. Fill in with rounder flowers and add foliage and trails. Don't forget to add water to the cones.

2

Make a tall cone of one inch mesh wire netting, filling this with wet moss. An alternative could be Oasis. Squeeze the lower end inserting it in vase, tying down if necessary. Wire small bunches of grapes, leaves, berries and roses, leaving a short false stem. Insert these wire stems into the moss giving a twist or bend to help them stay firm. Sprinkle the cone with water when finished.

3

Basic structure of arrangement on page 109.

4

Fill container with two inch mesh crumpled wire netting, making a cone shape with centre. Tie down to the vase with wire or string to avoid it slipping. Make the pattern of the arrangement with twigs, fine leaves or pointed flowers, and make sure some flow well forward over the rim in the front.

5

Insert more important flowers down the centre with the lower one protruding forward.

6

Fill in with medium sized flowers and unite all the stems at the centre with large leaves; add trails of ivy flowing downwards.

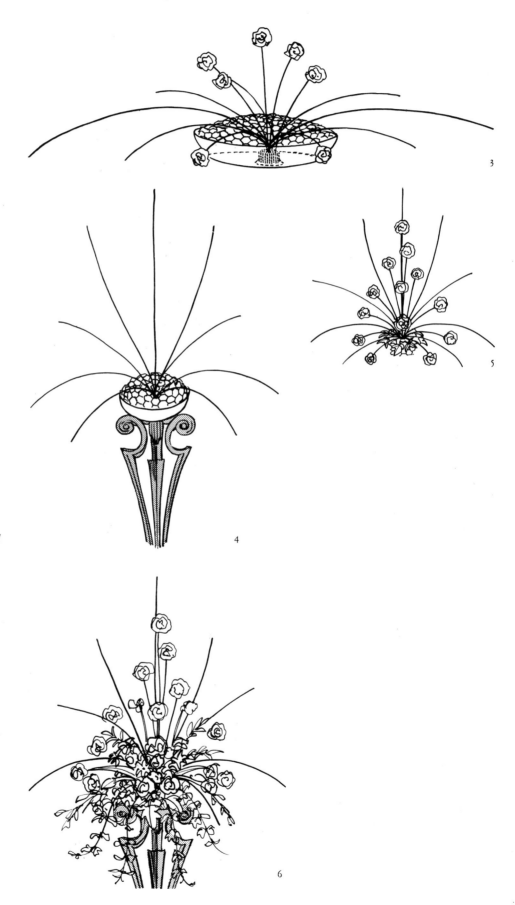

Further information on the houses and gardens mentioned in this book and times and dates of opening can be obtained locally or from the following : —

Historic Houses, Castles and Gardens
an annual publication from most stationers and bookstalls or direct from Index Publishers, 69 Victoria Street, London SW1

The National Gardens Scheme Guide Book
57 Lower Belgrave Street, London SW1

The National Trust list of Properties
42 Queen Anne's Gate, London SW1

British Travel & Holidays Association
64 St James's Street, London SW1

Scotland's Garden Scheme list
26 Castle Terrace, Edinburgh 1

Gardeners' Sunday
a list of Gardens open in aid of the Gardeners' Royal Benevolent Society and The Royal Gardeners' Orphan Fund. It is obtainable from Gardeners' Sunday, Four Winds, Seale, Farnham, Surrey